Young Millionaires
Secrets to Early Retirement

Table of Contents

Chapter 1. Introduction

Dreaming of a life untamed by the typical nine-to-five? Yearning for financial freedom to retire early and pursue your passions unabated? Maybe you're wondering how young millionaires have achieved such feats? If this resonates with you, our Special Report unlocks the secrets of these high achievers that have led them to early retirement. Filled with real-life success stories, actionable strategies, and valuable learnings that could potentially shape your financial journey, this report provides a roadmap to abundant wealth accumulation. It'll fuel your desire to take charge of your fate. Spring into early financial independence by diving into the secrets of young millionaires; because, why wait until 65 when you can redefine your possibilities today?

Chapter 2. Unlocking the Mindset of a Young Millionaire

Many people wonder how such young individuals are becoming millionaires and achieving financial independence at an age when many are just finding their place in the world. An exploration of their mindset, strategies, and patterns can provide insightful knowledge for individuals yearning to follow the same path of wealth accumulation and early retirement.

2.1. Psychological Perspective

One of the key differentiators between the typical individual and a young millionaire is their mindset—the most crucial being their attitude towards money. While many people perceive money as a necessity for survival, young millionaires look at money as a tool for creating more wealth. They see it as a stepping stone to greater financial freedom and independence—a concept that completely alters their approach towards earning and investing.

Young individuals who have scaled the lofty heights of wealth early in life are not afraid to take risks. Calculated and strategic, they are willing to step outside their comfort zones in the pursuit of big returns. A majority of these individuals have had early starts, often embarking on their entrepreneurial journey in their teens. This gives them a crucial advantage—time—that allows for learning from failures, capitalizing on their successes, and growing their investments.

2.2. Wealth Building Habits

While having a receptive mindset is essential, it's also the habits formed around this outlook that truly drive success for young millionaires. They invest a significant amount of their time and resources into learning, building, and maintaining their businesses. They don't hesitate to spend money where it counts, whether it's self-education, professional networking, or industry-specific tools and technology.

Young millionaires almost exclusively automate their savings and investments, ensuring that a portion of their income regularly fuels their wealth-growing engines without their direct intervention. This approach takes advantage of the power of compound interest—an essential tool for those aspiring to retire early and avoid the traditional 9-to-5 lifestyle.

2.3. Embracing Entrepreneurship

Entrepreneurship is the most common route to wealthy independence among young millionaires. They're not the ones contented with a regular pay job and saving little-by-little for their golden years. Instead, they often follow their passions, solve problems, and create products or services that offer utility to people—making money along the way. This entrepreneurial spirit lets them take control over their time, leverage their skills, and scale their income.

A common trait among young millionaires is their ability to see opportunities in problems. Rather than feeling bogged down by challenges they encounter, they seek innovative solutions to overcome these hurdles, often creating revenue from these problem-solving endeavors.

2.4. Investing In Real Estate

A common denominator in wealth building among young millionaires is their focus on real estate investments. By purchasing properties in emerging markets or renovating undervalued properties in established neighborhoods, they generate recurring rental income. This strategy provides both a regular income and an appreciating asset.

2.5. Diversifying Investments and Sources of Income

Young millionaires rarely have a single source of income. They invest in a variety of assets such as stocks, bonds, mutual funds, cryptocurrency, or private businesses. Such diverse investment not only amplifies their wealth but also provides a safety buffer during financial downturns.

Managing several sources of income isn't a task everyone is capable of. It requires discipline, balance, and a solid understanding of the different markets in which they invest. However, when executed successfully, it leads to significant diversification, risk mitigation, and potential return on investments.

2.6. Guiding Principles

Here are a few key principles that many young millionaires live by:

1. Achieving financial independence is more about mindset than material wealth.

2. Risk-taking is essential, but ensure risks are calculated and not haphazard gambles.

3. Invest in learning and personal development—it's the best

investment you can make.

4. Embrace entrepreneurship—it's the most direct path to financial independence.

5. Prioritize saving and investment—remember, compound interest is your best friend.

6. Diversify income sources to buffer against downturns and maximize potential growth.

7. Don't be afraid to see opportunities where others see problems.

Living by this mindset and these principles doesn't guarantee anyone will become a millionaire overnight—far from it. But they provide a roadmap to increase one's chances significantly, reducing the probability of getting stuck in the societal norm of working a regular job until 65. After all, life is an adventure, and taking charge of your financial destiny is an essential part of that journey.

Chapter 3. Building Wealth: Growth Tactics and Strategies

Building wealth is not a product of chance or luck, but rather, a result of meticulous planning, tactical decision-making, and strategic execution. This chapter will unveil some indispensable growth tactics and strategies adopted by young millionaires that you can emulate to kickstart or advance your wealth accumulation journey.

Let's begin unveiling the strategies:

3.1. Strategy 1: Hone Your Financial Literacy

Understanding money, and how it works, is a critical first step towards building your wealth. Financial literacy implies mastering the key concepts related with investing, saving, and budgeting. By boosting your financial literacy, you will be able to make more informed decisions that can positively drive your financial success.

Perhaps you're wondering about resources for this skill—consider any of these options:

- Books such as "Rich Dad, Poor Dad" by Robert Kiyosaki and "Think and Grow Rich" by Napoleon Hill

- Online courses from reputable platforms like Coursera, Udemy, and Khan Academy

- Podcasts and financial literacy blogs from finance experts

3.2. Strategy 2: Diversify Your Investments

Diversification protects you from the volatility of a single investment or asset class. Young millionaires often invest in a variety of assets, including stocks, bonds, real estate, and even startups or small businesses. This diversification is a safety net—they don't put all their eggs in one basket.

To diversify effectively:

- Analyze and understand the risk and returns associated with different investments

- Spread your investments across these different classes based on your financial goals and risk appetite

3.3. Strategy 3: Invest in Self And Skills

Investing in yourself is the best investment you could ever make. Enhancing your skills or learning new ones increases your earning potential—be it through promotions, raises, or freelance gigs. Consider investing in educational courses, acquiring relevant certifications, or learning new languages. Such self-improvement catapults your career and ultimately your wealth.

3.4. Strategy 4: Develop Multiple Income Streams

The concept of multiple income streams has gained great popularity among young millionaires. Having more than one source of income not only mitigates financial risks but also accelerates wealth accumulation. These streams could stem from rentals, dividends from investments, side businesses, or freelance work.

3.5. Strategy 5: Aim for High Income Skills

High income skills are abilities that can generate substantial income—usually upwards of $10,000 per month. Examples include: digital marketing, copywriting, programming, consulting, and sales. Hone one of these, and it could be your game-changing ticket to rapid wealth build-up.

3.6. Strategy 6: Leverage The Power of Compound Interest

Albert Einstein once referred to compound interest as "the eighth wonder of the world," illustrating its extraordinary power in wealth accumulation. With compound interest, your wealth grows exponentially, since interest is calculated on the initial principal and also on the accumulated interest from previous periods.

To take advantage of this:

- Start investing early—every year counts

- Reinvest your earnings to gain interest on them as well

- Let your investments grow untouched for years or even decades

3.7. Strategy 7: Live Below Your Means

Wealth is not about how much you earn, but rather, how much you keep. By living below your means, you'll be able to accumulate wealth while avoiding unnecessary financial stress—with the added money, you can invest more and save more.

Be guided by these tips:

- Craft and follow a realistic budget

- Differentiate between what you need and what you want—prioritize necessities

- Avoid debts or pay them off as soon as possible to reduce unnecessary interests

3.8. Strategy 8: Network Effectively

Your social network can be your most powerful asset. Surrounding yourself with ambitious, successful people can inspire new ideas, offer opportunities, and create valuable partnerships. Remember, building wealth often comes from the right opportunities—and the right people can provide them. Attend industry events, utilize social media, and embrace networking.

These strategies are not a one-size-fits-all solution but are replicable models of success. Strategically implementing them according to your unique financial circumstance and future goals can serve as a powerful catalyst for wealth accumulation. Visualize the life you desire, commit to your financial journey, and watch as these strategies bring you closer to your financial freedom.

Chapter 4. The Power of Compound Interest and Early Investing

Not everyone has experienced the thrill of seeing their account balance exponentially grow from smart investing strategies. But those who have will tell you that this phenomenon boils down to the 'Eighth Wonder of the World': compound interest. Specifically, when you start investing early with the power of compound interest, you can amass a formidable fortune, setting the stage for potential early retirement.

4.1. Understanding Compound Interest

Albert Einstein famously quipped, "Those who understand interest earn it, those who don't, pay it." Compound interest is essentially "interest on interest." It's the result of reinvesting interest, rather than paying it out, so that interest in the next period is earned on the principal sum plus previously accumulated interest. In other words, when your investments earn interest, this amount gets reinvested, which in turn earns even more interest.

To truly grasp the power of compound interest, let's consider the following example. Say you invest $1,000 at an annual interest rate of 5%. In the first year, you'd earn $50 in interest. The next year, you're not just earning 5% on your initial $1,000, but also the $50 in interest you gained, putting the year's total at $1,052.50. Over time, the interest accumulates, leading to a snowball effect wherein the amount being accumulated continues to grow, hence its powerful impact.

4.2. The Time Value of Money

The concept of compound interest goes hand in hand with the 'Time Value of Money'. This economic principle suggests that the money available at the present time is worth more than an identical sum in the future due to its potential capacity to earn interest. In other words, money in the bank today is better than money in the bank tomorrow.

The formula for compound interest, $A = P(1 + r/n)^{(nt)}$, where A is the money accumulated after n years, including interest; P is the principal amount (the initial amount you invest); r is the annual interest rate (in decimal); n is the number of times interest is applied per year; t is the time the money is invested for, in years, helps us understand the relationship between compound interest and time.

Simply put, the longer the time period that the money is invested, the more the interest-on-interest effect can play out, enabling the exponential growth of wealth. Essentially, time can be viewed as the secret ingredient in this financial recipe. The 'n' in the formula demonstrates that the compounding effect is exponential - the larger the 'n', the higher the final amount.

4.3. Early Investing: The Key To Exponential Wealth

It's not just about investing, but investing early. Time in the market concerns how long you hold onto your investments, and this is a crucial factor in wealth accumulation. The stock market can be unpredictable in the short run, but it has historically trended upward in the long term. This is especially potent in the context of compound interest.

Consider our earlier example — if you invested $1,000 and waited ten years instead of one to calculate interest, the outcome, even at a

5% interest rate, would be substantially higher. And if you were continually contributing more to this investment over those ten years, the result would be multiplied many times over.

Let's illustrate this by introducing two investors, Alice and Bob. Alice began investing at the age of 25, placing $300 into a retirement account each month at an average annual return rate of 7%. Meanwhile, Bob started investing at 35 under the same conditions. By the time they reach 65, Alice would have invested $144,000, while Bob would have invested $108,000. However, due to the power of compound interest and early investing, Alice's account would be approximately $739,120, while Bob's would only be about $373,407.

This makes a clear case for the importance of early investing. The extra ten years Alice had, allowed compound interest to significantly increase her account balance, even though she only invested $36,000 more than Bob.

4.4. Making Compound Interest and Early Investing Work for You

Understanding the power of compound interest and the importance of early investing is the first step; now, you need to act. You can take advantage of individual retirement accounts (IRAs), employer sponsored plans like 401(k)s or Personal Savings Accounts (PSA), index funds, or other investment portfolios to get started. Remember, the road to financial independence and early retirement isn't about timing the market but rather spending time in the market.

Ever wondered how young millionaires find their road to early retirement? The secret isn't an enigma – it's simply understanding the power of compound interest and the advantage of early investing. As demonstrated by Alice's success story, an extra ten years could potentially mean an extra $365,713 in your retirement account. Your journey to financial freedom might just be a wise investment strategy away.

Chapter 5. Real Estate Revelations: Investment and Revenue

Many young millionaires have made their fortune by investing wisely in Real Estate. They successfully maneuvered this dynamic market by following a disciplined approach and meticulosly strategizing their steps. This chapter uncovers their secrets and offers actionable strategies to help you on your journey towards financial freedom.

5.1. Understanding Real Estate Investment

Real estate is a tangible asset that has always held its worth, providing an excellent investment option that promises better appreciation over time, as well as stable income through rent or lease. To some, the prospect of investing in real estate can seem daunting due to high capital requirements and uncertainty in market trends. However, young millionaires have rocketed past these fears by seeing real estate for what it truly is: an investment with huge potential for generating passive income.

An engaged approach to real estate investment demands understanding market trends, appreciating the location's potential, calculating potential returns, and knowing when to buy or sell the property.

5.2. Building a Solid Foundation

Before jumping into purchasing your first property, you need to build a solid foundation. This means organizing your personal finances, improving your credit score, and securing pre-approval for a mortgage. Young millionaires emphasize the importance of a strong financial foundation before initiating real estate transactions. Your financial capacity determines how many properties you can acquire, and knowing your budget upfront allows you to make strategic purchasing decisions.

5.3. Choosing the Right Investment: Rental Properties

One of the most popular ways young millionaires generate passive income is by investing in rental properties. Whether single-family homes, duplexes, apartments, or commercial properties, these investments provide a steady revenue stream.

However, it's not all about collecting rent; understanding your duties as a landlord also matters. From property maintenance to rent collection and dealing with tenants, handling a rental property demands time and patience.

5.4. Diving into 'Buy-and-Hold' Investments

A popular investment strategy among young millionaires is buying and holding properties. They recognize that real estate is a long-term game, and patience is key.

These investors buy properties with the intent to keep them for many years, reaping considerable benefits in the process. Over time, property values appreciate, and when the time is right, selling can result in a substantial profit.

5.5. Flipping Properties for Profit

Flipping properties involves buying a distressed property, renovating it, and selling it for profit. This strategy is riskier but can offer higher short-term returns if executed correctly.

Young millionaires do so by understanding the market inside out, recognizing the potential of a property, and having a keen eye for renovation costs. Patience and market understanding play an integral role in this strategy.

5.6. Exploring Real Estate Investment Trusts (REITs)

Not all young millionaires attained their fortune through physical properties. Some have found considerable wealth by investing in REITs. It involves purchasing shares of companies that own and operate income-generating real estate. This strategy offers flexibility and allows a hands-off approach to real estate investment, with benefits of liquidity and dividend income.

5.7. Investing in Vacation Rental Properties

Vacation rental properties have revolutionized traditional real estate investment in recent years. Sites like Airbnb have made it possible for property owners to generate substantial income from their properties.

These properties can be rented out when not in use providing a consistent income stream. Savvy investors see the potential of vacation hotspots and capitalize on tourist seasons to maximize their profits.

5.8. Commercial Real Estate Investments

While most associate real estate with residential properties, commercial real estate investments have powerful potential. These are properties that house businesses, like office buildings, retail stores, and industrial warehousing.

While the cost of entry is high, so is the potential return. Rent contracts tend to be longer, providing a secure revenue stream. Plus, commercial tenants often take on some of the property maintenance responsibilities, reducing landlord overheads.

5.9. Risks and Mitigation

While the benefits are plentiful, young millionaires also recognize that real estate investment comes with risks. Market fluctuations, unexpected expenses, challenging tenants, and legal complications are just some of the potential pitfalls. That's why they always stress the importance of due diligence, adequate insurance, legal assistance, and emergency funds to cope with unforeseen expenses.

5.10. Creating a Real Estate Network

Having a network of professionals can make navigating the real estate market easier. This network can include realtors, lawyers, contractors, property managers, and fellow investment property owners.

These relationships are instrumental, and young millionaires leverage them both for advice and timely opportunities.

This chapter only scratches the surface of real estate investment. But what can be discerned from the strategies and wisdom of young millionaires is that success hinges on a combination of knowledge, networking, due diligence, patience, and resilience. With the correct approach and mindset, real estate investment can certainly pave your path to early retirement.

Chapter 6. Startup Success Stories: Turning Ideas Into Fortunes

The entrepreneurial journey is thrilling and rife with challenges, but it can also lead to substantial financial rewards - an aspect that has enticed many young individuals to pursue this path. Let's dive deep into the incredible startup success stories that transformed ideas into fortunes.

6.1. The Airbnb Journey

In 2007, roommates Brian Chesky and Joe Gebbia couldn't afford the rent for their San Francisco apartment. To make ends meet, they turned their living room into a makeshift bed and breakfast for attendees of a large local conference. Within a year, they teamed up with Nathan Blecharczyk to launch Airbnb.

Fast-forward to present day, Airbnb has revolutionized the way people travel and find accommodations around the world. It's now a global giant valued at approximately $100 billion, and its founders are among the world's youngest billionaires.

Key takeaway: With a combination of innovative concepts, sufficient market research, and determination, great ideas can genuinely become global game-changers.

6.2. Spanx: A Billion-dollar Undergarment Business

In the late nineties, Sara Blakely was selling fax machines door-to-door. Then one day, in search of a flattering undergarment for her white pants, she cut the feet off her pantyhose. This sparked the idea for Spanx, a women's apparel company that specializes in shapewear. Blakely launched Spanx in 2000 with her savings of $5000 without any background in fashion or retail.

By 2012, she became the world's youngest self-made female billionaire, with Spanx being sold in over 65 countries. Today, Blakely still owns 100% of her company.

Key takeaway: Passion, resilience, and self-belief, matched with an idea that meets a market demand, can lead to monumental success.

6.3. The Snapchat Saga

Snapchat, an ephemeral photo messaging app, was created by Evan Spiegel, Bobby Murphy, and Reggie Brown while they were students at Stanford University. Despite initial skepticism because of its disappearing content premise, Snapchat rapidly gained popularity among young users and became a new communication norm.

Snap Inc. was valued at nearly $33 billion on its first day of trading on the NYSE in 2017. The co-founders, still in their 20s at the time, joined the lists of the world's youngest billionaires.

Key takeaway: With technological advancements and changing market desires, unconventional ideas can disrupt the status quo and lead to tremendous financial success.

6.4. The Shopify Success Story

In 2004, Tobias Lütke and Scott Lake, aiming to sell snowboards online, were unsatisfied with the e-commerce products available. So, they decided to build their own. This idea laid the foundation for Shopify, a platform designed to make selling online accessible for small business owners.

Presently, Shopify, worth over $130 billion, powers over a million businesses in 175 countries. Co-founder and CEO, Lütke, is involved in policy councils influencing U.S. and Canadian economic strategies.

Key takeaway: In problem-solving lies the potential to create a product that could benefit a wider audience and result in financial success.

It is important to note that not every venture is a rousing success. Many entrepreneurs experience failure before they find success. However, stories like these demonstrate the role of startups in economic growth and job creation, and they highlight the power of innovative thinking combined with strategic planning. In the domain of financial independence and entrepreneurship, there is no one-size-fits-all approach, but these stories offer inspiration and practical insights on the path from ideas to fortune.

Chapter 7. Balancing Risk and Reward: The Millionaire's Tightrope

There are few endeavors in life where the balance between risk and reward becomes as palpable as it does in wealth creation. Embracing the correct degree of manageable risks can potentially rocket you towards your financial goals. However, an ill-advised risk can also result in devastating losses. It isn't a secret recipe known to only a fraction of the population. Rather, it's a walk down a thin rope where every step demands acute consciousness about the perilous drop on either side.

7.1. The Daredevil Approach

Successful investing is often compared to walking on a tightrope, where the performer's survival wholly depends upon maintaining a steady balance. It's not about eliminating the risk – highly improbable in the financial landscape – but it's about handling and controlling it meticulously. Wandering too far on either side of this tightrope is detrimental – extreme conservatism will stunt growth whilst too much aggression can lead to catastrophic losses. Young millionaires have mastered this delicate balancing act, enabling them to create massive fortunes.

A "daredevil" investment approach might tantalize some, encouraged by the promise of quick, rich returns. Highly speculative investments such as low-cap penny stocks, high-leverage Foreign Exchange trades, or emerging cryptocurrencies might hold the potential for exponential growth. Nevertheless, bear in mind that these opportunities are associated with equally profound risks. Cases of investors losing their entire capital are far too common.

Subtler dangers lurk here as well - addiction to the thrill of high-stakes trading and living on the edge can detract from logical, disciplined investing. It's crucial to remember that investing is not a game but a vehicle for wealth accumulation and preservation. Short-term wins may be exhilarating, yet financial independence is a long-term endeavor.

7.2. Conservative Doesn't Mean Cowardly

On the other hand, adopting a too-conservative approach can also be detrimental. Investments in extremely low-risk assets invariably lead to insufficient growth over the long haul. This is often caused by an irrational fear of losses, lack of knowledge, or due to being burnt by past failures. Avoiding all risks might seem tempting, but it essentially ensures mediocrity.

Take, for example, placing all your savings in a low-interest savings account. You'll experience the safety of your capital growing, albeit at a snail's pace. This approach overlooks the eroding power of inflation, which, if higher than the interest you're receiving, means you're losing money in real terms. Financially successful individuals understand that the courageous don't avoid risk; instead, they befriend it, measure it, and exploit it to their advantage.

7.3. Strategic Risk Taking

Millionaires understand that risk is inherent to growth. They don't shy away from opportunities due to fear of failure. Instead, they allocate a section of their portfolio for calculated risk-taking.

This strategy involves thorough research, identifying high-potential investments with decent risk/reward ratios, and committing a manageable sum. If the investment thrives, it could bring significant returns, and if it doesn't, the loss won't be crippling. Diversification across numerous such opportunities can further optimize this approach, as the success of some can counterbalance failures, smoothing out overall portfolio performance.

7.4. Risk Management: The Safety Net

Risk can't be entirely avoided. This inevitability forces us to deploy robust risk management strategies to protect our wealth. These include:

1. Set clear investment goals and align them with your risk tolerance.

2. Regularly review and adjust your investment portfolio, factoring in changes in the market or personal circumstances.

3. Diversify across multiple asset classes, geographies, and sectors to spread risk.

4. Maintain an emergency fund to ride out unpredictable market downturns without needing to liquidate investments at an inopportune time.

5. Regularly rebalance your portfolio to maintain your desired risk/reward ratio.

These strategies constitute the safety net under the tightrope, reducing the potential impact of a fall.

7.5. Embrace the Growth Mindset

Finally, the journey to financial independence requires a growth mindset. This involves recognizing that failures and setbacks are an integral part of the journey. Rather than being deterred by them, they provide opportunities for learning and refining strategies. Many self-made millionaires attest that their greatest lessons and turning points came from their most distressing failures.

Risk is a formidable challenge on the journey to financial independence. It is unpredictable, baring its teeth when least expected. However, a judicious approach to risk and reward, courage in the face of uncertainty, and a robust risk management framework can ensure stellar financial growth. Embrace the test of the tightrope with poise and resilience; after all, it might just be the thrilling financial journey you've been seeking.

Chapter 8. Decoding the Stock Market: A Millennial's Guide

Investing in the stock market can seem like a daunting task, especially for those who are new to it. Yet, it remains one of the most effective ways to accumulate substantial wealth, provided it is approached with prudence, respect, and a larger understanding.

8.1. Knowing the Basics

Before diving deep into strategies and technicalities, it's crucial to understand the fundamental concepts related to the stock market. Stocks, also known as shares, represent a piece of ownership in a corporation. When you buy a stock, you essentially buy a small fraction of that company. Companies issue stocks to raise funds for different purposes - for expansion, to pay off debt, or merely to diversify their capital structure.

The stock market refers to the collection of markets and exchanges where activities of buying, selling, and issuance of shares take place. Two of the best-known markets globally are the New York Stock Exchange (NYSE) and the NASDAQ.

8.2. The Importance of Diversification

One of the critical principles that young millionaires swear by is the power of diversification. As the saying goes, "Don't put all your eggs in one basket."

The goal of diversification is to invest in various assets so that a loss in one security doesn't significantly impact the entire investment portfolio. According to Modern Portfolio Theory, an investor can reap higher returns by investing in a diversified portfolio of multiple non-correlated assets.

8.3. Understanding Risk vs. Reward

Every investment comes with an inherent risk. Hence, before making any investment decision, it's essential to understand the risk-reward ratio - the potential for loss versus the potential for growth.

Generally, high-risk assets have the potential for higher returns but also higher potential losses. Low-risk assets, on the other hand, offer lower returns but with less likelihood of significant losses. In the stock market, companies with high growth potential are often categorized as high-risk investments, while blue-chip companies, known for their stable earnings, are considered low-risk investments.

8.4. The Power of Compounding

One of the profound secrets of young millionaires is their understanding and leveraging the power of compounding. Compounding, at its core, is the process of generating earnings on an asset's reinvested earnings. Over time, as investments continue to earn returns, the invested capital begins to mushroom.

The key to effective compounding is starting as early as possible. Einstein once reportedly said, "Compounding is the eighth wonder of the world. He who understands it earns it. He who doesn't, pays it." By starting early, you provide your assets with more time to grow.

8.5. Long-Term Investing vs. Short-term Trading

Broadly, there are two approaches to the stock market - long-term investing and short-term trading.

Long-term investors buy stocks with an aim to hold them for many years, often decades. They primarily focus on companies with solid growth potential over time. This strategy is heavily based on fundamental analysis, a method of evaluating a security to measure its intrinsic value by examining macroeconomic and company-specific factors.

Short-term trading, including day trading or swing trading, relies more heavily on technical analysis. These traders try to profit from market volatility by buying and selling stocks within shorter time frames.

While both approaches have their pros and cons, most successful young millionaires favor long-term investing because it's generally less risky and more predictable. It's essential for beginners to educate themselves thoroughly before taking up trading due to its risky nature.

8.6. Research: Your Power Tool

No one should invest in any stock based solely on tips from friends, family, or so-called market gurus. Every successful investor conducts thorough research and analysis before putting their money into any stock.

This research can entail studying a company's financial health, its management quality, the industry in which it operates, and its competitive landscape. It's also necessary to understand global economic factors and how they can affect the stock market.

In this digital age, multiple websites and platforms provide real-time data, news updates, and detailed analysis to aid investors in their research work. Some of the popular ones are Yahoo Finance, Google Finance, Bloomberg, and Morningstar.

8.7. Stay Disciplined and Patient

Stock market investing is not a 'get-rich-quick' scheme. It requires patience, discipline, and consistency. There might be periods of high volatility, where the market might test your patience. Rather than making hasty decisions during such periods, successful investors stick to their investing plans and strategies.

Remember, the journey to becoming a millionaire is not an overnight phenomenon. It's about making consistent investing decisions, regularly saving, and maintaining discipline over a longer period.

To conclude, investing in the stock market can be a rewarding journey if approached with the correct knowledge and understanding. Do your due diligence, have patience, and be consistent. Who knows? You might be the next millionaire sharing your success story!

Chapter 9. The Role of Networking & Mentorship in Wealth Creation

The paramountcy of networking and mentorship in wealth creation cannot be overstated. It's through the symbiotic relation of giving and receiving in these spheres that opportunities for wealth accumulation manifest.

9.1. Understanding Networking

Networking, in layman's terms, means creating and nurturing relationships that offer mutual value. It's about bridging gaps between your capabilities and opportunities, which you might not be aware of otherwise. It's the gateway to new ideas, experiences, and perspectives that could catalyze your journey towards wealth accumulation.

In fact, research shows that around 85% of all jobs are filled through networking. Successful entrepreneurs or business magnates, like Elon Musk or Tim Ferris, have leveraged their network for capital, business partners, or customers, which are all essential elements for wealth accumulation.

Successful networking isn't just about acquiring contacts; it's about building relationships. It involves proactively reaching out to people, learning from them, being open to opportunities, and providing value in return.

Let's illuminate this concept with a real-life example. Reid Hoffman, co-founder of LinkedIn and a member of the PayPal Mafia, was known for keeping elaborate spreadsheets to manage his relationships. He leveraged these relationships to get introductions, find partners, and gather resources for his ventures.

9.2. The Power of Mentorship

While networking broadens your horizons, it's the mentorship that gives you a compass - a direction towards wealth creation. Mentorship offers a chance to learn from individuals who have already walked the path you wish to embark on, providing insights from their victories and mistakes.

An essential facet of mentorship is the application of proven strategies and wisdom, which other might have toiled for years to acquire. It's about leveraging the skills, knowledge, and experience of a mentor to fast-track your journey of wealth creation.

Think about Elon Musk and how he cites Robert Heinlein's science fiction novels as an influence on his vision for SpaceX. Similarly, Jeff Bezos, founder of Amazon, mentions his grandfather as a mentor who cultivated his sense of resourcefulness and self-reliance.

9.3. Networking & Mentorship: A Combination for Wealth Creation

While networking creates possibilities, mentorship provides the knowledge and guidance to explore those possibilities effectively. Let's look at Mark Zuckerberg, Facebook's co-founder. Zuckerberg was introduced to Peter Thiel, co-founder of PayPal, through Reid Hoffman's network. This introduction led to Thiel's early investment in Facebook, and the rest, as we know, is history.

Business ventures, investments, and career advancements created through networks and enhanced by mentorship can lead to significant wealth accumulation.

9.4. Networking Strategies for Wealth Creation

While understanding the impact of networking is essential, knowing how to network effectively is the key.

1. **Be Proactive:** Don't wait for opportunities to come knocking; rather, reach out to people in your industry, attend conferences, and actively participate in forums.

2. **Provide Value:** Instead of only seeking help, provide something of value. This two-way street builds more robust and long-lasting relationships.

3. **Leverage Social Media:** It's an excellent tool to reach like-minded professionals across the globe. LinkedIn, Twitter, and even Instagram can be excellent sources for networking.

Each of these strategies has the potential to open doors and create wealth-building opportunities.

9.5. Leveraging Mentorship for Wealth Creation

Here are some strategies that can help leverage mentorship effectively.

1. **Selecting the Right Mentor:** Choose a mentor whose success mirrors your aspirations. Their journey, learnings, and methodologies will be most relevant to you.

2. **Actively Listen and Learn:** A mentor's guidance is most effective when absorbed and applied. Seek their advice and act on it to gain the most benefit.

3. **Engage Regularly:** Regular engagement helps to maintain the

relationship and continue learning from your mentor's evolving experiences.

Both networking and mentorship are not one-time activities, but rather ongoing processes. Creating and nurturing these relationships requires time, effort, and patience. But, when employed effectively, they could be the most potent tools for building the immense wealth that you aspire for. Therefore, plunge into this journey of networking and mentorship, learn, grow, and let the wealth follow. It's worthwhile to remember that your network is your net worth.

Chapter 10. Life Beyond 9-to-5: Sustainable Passive Income Streams

While many of us equate wealth creation to being tethered to a tight-knit corporate schedule, there is an entire world of financial opportunities that don't subscribe to this mindset. Our day-to-day lives exist far beyond the confines of a predictable structure, flushing out the common trope that success is coupled with long office hours. Instead, let's explore the intersection of wealth creation with freedom and flexibility—specifically through the lens of sustainable passive income streams.

10.1. Understanding Passive Income

At its core, passive income is earnings one acquires without actively toiling for it on a regular schedule. Sounds enticing, doesn't it? The concept revolves around creating systems—be they investments, projects, or businesses—that yield consistent returns without demanding a proportional amount of your time. But before we delve into these ventures let us differentiate between active and passive income, providing a foundational understanding to comprehend the ensuing strategies.

Active income refers to a paycheck: money you earn in direct proportion to the hours you work. This includes salaries, wages, and tips. Think of your nine-to-five job. For many, the primary downside of active income is its linear nature: if you don't work, you don't earn.

In contrast, passive income represents earnings from sources one does not materially participate in. This can range vastly, from rental income to earnings from investments, royalties from a book you wrote, or sales from an online course. While it requires upfront effort and investment, the payoff continually trickles into your pocket with minimal ongoing work.

10.2. The Pillars of Passive Income

There are several avenues to generate passive income, each with its strengths, weaknesses, requirements, and levels of involvements. Common misconceptions frame passive income as a quick win or an effortless cash-grab; in contrast, most passive income streams require a significant upfront investment, be that time, capital, or both. However, once the system is set-up and operational, the maintenance required scales down drastically.

We will now explore four of these avenues striking the most successful balance between effort and reward: Investment in Stocks & Bonds, Real Estate Investment, Creating Digital Assets, and Peer-to-Peer Lending.

10.3. Investment in Stocks & Bonds

Stock and bond investments are one of the longest-standing and most widely accepted forms of passive income. In simple terms, buying a share of a stock means buying a small piece of that company. Stocks generate income in two key ways: dividends and capital gains.

Dividends are portions of a company's profit directly paid to shareholders. It's an immediate return on your investment, independent of the stock's market value. Not all companies provide dividends, principally those in growth phases, reinvesting profits to fuel expansion.

Capital gains refer to increased stock value over time. The idea is to buy stocks at a low price and sell them when the price appreciates. However, predicting market trends requires substantial knowledge and has inherent risks, which underscores the importance of having a diversified investment portfolio.

On the other hand, bonds are debt instruments. Governments, municipalities, or corporations issue bonds to raise capital, promising to pay back the original amount plus interest after a specific period.

The compounding nature of these investments makes them attractive for those seeking long-term wealth accumulation. Initial capital, rates of return, and reinvestment strategies impact your earnings substantially—making it crucial to research, consult professionals, and invest consciously.

10.4. Real Estate Investment

Investing in real estate is a tangible way of generating passive income. There are different ways to go about this: rental properties, Real Estate Investment Trusts (REITs), and crowdfunded real estate investing.

Rental properties promise a regular income stream, assuming they're occupied by tenants. However, they demand initial capital, property management skills (or hiring someone who does), and finding reliable tenants.

REITs are like mutual funds for real estate, allowing you to invest in large-scale properties like shopping malls or commercial buildings. REITs are legally mandated to distribute 90% of their taxable profits to investors in the form of dividends, leading to consistent income.

Crowdfunding platforms are a recent addition, requiring less capital than direct real estate investments. These platforms pool investors' money to fund properties, distributing the returns proportionately.

10.5. Creating Digital Assets

If you possess a skill, knowledge, or passion, you can turn it into a revenue-generating digital asset.

Creating and selling online courses, subscription services, ebooks, or webinars can tap into the global digital market. Similarly, monetizing a blog or YouTube channel through advertising revenue or sponsorships can generate a stable income trickle if you create engaging content that resonates with your audience.

Additionally, if you hold expertise in graphic design or photography, you might consider selling digital files on platforms like Etsy or Shutterstock.

Remember, creating digital assets requires a significant initial time investment and usually a serendipitous blend of marketing acumen, quality content creation, and timing. However, with the right blend and persistence, it becomes a truly passive playground.

10.6. Peer-to-Peer Lending

With the democratisation of finance thanks to technology, Peer-to-Peer (P2P) lending platforms connect investors with borrowers directly, bypassing traditional financial institutions.

As an investor on these platforms, you extend loans to individuals or small businesses in return for interest payments. The risk varies, dependent on the platform, borrowers' creditworthiness, and loan diversification. However, the return rates are often higher than traditional bonds or high-yield savings accounts.

While it seems effortless, it's essential to research different P2P platforms, their risk policies, and default rates. Local regulations and the novelty of this domain add an extra layer of considerations.

10.7. Turning the Wheel: From Active to Passive

Transitioning from an active to passive revenue structure demands a well-thought-out strategy, starting with saving and investing wisely during your active income years. Prioritize creating an emergency fund, clearing off high-interest debts, and then invest in diverse income-generating assets, opting for strategies fitting your risk tolerance and financial goals.

Implementing these strategies will require learning, consulting experts, and making some mistakes. But, as annual reports and success stories attest, the transformation leads to amplified earnings, reduced active work periods, and ultimately, financial independence.

Remember, passive income does not mean no effort; it means delayed gratification, converting today's efforts into tomorrow's ongoing returns. It urges you to look beyond the immediate, envision the potential, and enact the path to financial freedom, taking control of your time and fate, one investment at a time.

The idea is not to escape work but to create a life that doesn't revolve around it. Thus, passive income is just as much about financial independence as it is about liberating yourself to invest your time more meaningfully. Establishing sustainable passive income streams pushes you beyond a life trapped within a 9-to-5 framework, paving a path to pursue passions unabated and retire early, shaping the future you desire, not one dictated by financial constraints.

Chapter 11. Staying Wealthy: Managing and Maintaining Your Fortune

Financial success story doesn't end once you have built a substantial fortune. It's the starting line for a new journey—one that involves preserving and growing the accumulated wealth responsibly, with a focus on long-term fiscal stability.

11.1. Understanding Wealth Management

First and foremost, comprehending wealth management is essential. Wealth management isn't solely about solid investment decisions. It's a holistic approach to financial health, covering everything from tax planning, estate planning, to managing investments and insurance. Through effective wealth management, you preserve prosperity and promise future growth.

11.2. Investments: Diversification is Key

The linchpin of wealth management is investing, and here, diversification is crucial. Having a spread of investments across diverse assets and sectors mitigates risks and boosts returns. From equities, bonds, real estate, commodities, to even new-age categories like cryptocurrencies, striking a healthy balance between various asset classes will help steady your fortune against market volatility.

You may want to consider different geographic markets as well. Diversification can span across industries and borders. Focusing on a variety of growth-potential and mature economies affords a blend of stability and growth, cushioning your wealth against regional economic downturns.

Additionally, remember that passive income sources through investment play a significant role in maintaining your fortune. Dividends from equities, rent from real estate holdings, and interest from bonds can add to a steady income stream, ensuring your wealth continues to grow even as you enjoy your early retirement.

11.3. Risk Management: Protecting Your Investments

While investing for growth is necessary, it's equally paramount to safeguard your wealth. Through proper risk management, you prevent significant losses during turbulent times. This includes setting stop losses in volatile markets and having a solid insurance policy to save your wealth from potential future liabilities.

One aspect of risk management is ensuring that your investments appropriately match your risk appetite. Carefully evaluate each investment for risk versus return, maintaining a blend that aligns with your comfort zone and financial goals.

11.4. Tax Planning: Minimize Your Liabilities

Taxation is an area that's often overlooked by many when managing wealth. It could easily eat into your profits if not properly planned. Seek advice from tax professionals and opt for tax-efficient investments that complement your financial goals.

A well-crafted tax strategy involves maximizing your use of tax exemptions, deductions, and credits. The use of tax-advantaged retirement accounts, strategic charitable giving, and careful estate planning can significantly reduce your tax burden.

11.5. Estate Planning: Leaving a Legacy

A wealth management plan isn't complete without addressing estate planning. Developing a clear and robust estate plan ensures your wealth is transferred as per your wishes and minimizes the tax burden on your heirs. This involves creating a will, determining powers of attorney, and considering trust structures.

Transferring wealth might also involve gifting assets during your lifetime, which might have tax implications. Working with a professional estate planner can help navigate these complexities.

11.6. Regular Monitoring and Review

Finally, staying wealthy is about regular monitoring and continual adaptations. The economic environment and regulations change; so must your wealth management strategy. Regular reviews will ensure your strategy stays relevant and effective.

Simply amassing a fortune isn't an endpoint. It's the commencement of a journey to safeguard and expand that wealth. By managing your investments, mitigating risks, planning for taxes, foreseeing estate issues, and making regular reviews and adaptations, you can maintain your fortune, ensuring a sustainable, wealthy life. Remember, wealth management is not a one-time act, but a lifelong journey that dictates how well you preserve your hard-earned wealth for your future generations and causes.

www.ingramcontent.com/pod-product-compliance
Lightning Source LLC
Chambersburg PA
CBHW071039260726
48661CB00007B/3066